# Spin, Weave, Knit and Knot

### Cheryl Jakab

THOMSON
━━━━━★━━━━━
NELSON

**PM Extras Non-fiction Emerald Level**

How Does Your Garden Grow?
Working with Wood
How Magic Tricks Work
Junk Sculpture
Spin, Weave, Knit and Knot
The Puppet Show

**PM Extras Non-fiction**
Emerald Level

PM Extras is published by Thomson Learning Australia and is distributed as follows:

AUSTRALIA
Thomson Learning
102 Dodds Street
Southbank 3006
Victoria

NEW ZEALAND
Nelson Price Milburn
1 Te Puni Street
Petone
Wellington

First published in 2004
10 9 8 7 6 5 4 3 2 1
08 07 06 05 04

Text © 2004 Nelson Australia Pty Ltd
Illustrations © 2004 Nelson Australia Pty Ltd

Spin, Weave, Knit and Knot
ISBN 0 17 011440 6
ISBN 0 17 011434 1 (set)

Illustrations by Georgie Wilson
Edited by Angelique Campbell-Muir
Designed by Georgie Wilson
Printed in China by Midas Printing (Asia) Ltd

Nelson Australia Pty Limited ACN 058 280 149 (incorporated in Victoria) trading as
Thomson Learning Australia.

Email: nelson@thomsonlearning.com.au
Website: www.thomsonlearning.com.au

Acknowledgements:
The author and publisher would like to acknowledge permission to reproduce material
from the following sources:
Photographs by The Art Archive/ Musée du Lourve Paris/ Dagli Orti, p. 18 bottom/
Topkapi Museum Istanbul/ Dagli Orti, p. 22 right; Australian Picture Library/ Corbis/
Christie's Images, p. 22 left/ Lindsay Hebberd, p. 7 left/ Dave G. Houser, p. 8 right/ Hulton
Deutsch Collection, p. 19 top/ Jacqui Hurst, pp. 4 centre, 13/ Tim Kiusalaas, p. 5 bottom
left/ Kevin R. Morris, p. 9/ Richard T. Nowitz, p. 7 right/ Gianni Dagli Orti, p. 18 top/ Jose
Luis Pelaez, Inc., p. 12/ Science Pictures Limited, pp. 6 top right, 6 bottom left, 6 bottom
right/ Reproduced by permission of The State Hermitage Museum, St. Petersburg, Russia,
p. 23 top right/ David H. Wells, p. 4 right/ Jim Zuckerman, p. 6 top left; Coo-ee Picture
Library, pp. 19 bottom left, 19 bottom right; Getty Images/ Stone, p. 23/ Taxi, front cover
top, back cover, pp. 4 left, 5 top left, 5 right; Newspix, front cover bottom, pp. 17 left, 17
right/ Stuart McEvoy, p. 16/ Craig Mitchell, p. 15; Photodisc, pp. 3, 8 left, 23 top left; Irina
Serbina/ www.macrameboutique.com, p. 20.

# Contents

# Chapter 1

## About fibres and fabrics

**Fibres** are all around us. Look closely at the clothes you are wearing. You will see they are made with fibres. Some fibres are used as threads for sewing and other fibres are made into fabrics.

Balls of wool.

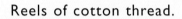

Reels of cotton thread.

Rolls of fabric.

Fibres can come from many different sources. Some fibres, such as wool and silk, come from animals. Some fibres, such as cotton, come from plants. These are all **natural** fibres, and have been used to make clothing for thousands of years.

Some fibres, such as nylon and polyester, are made from chemicals. These are called **synthetic** fibres. Synthetic fibres were first produced in the 1900s. They are cheaper and easier to produce than natural fibres.

# Using threads, fibres and fabrics

People have discovered many different ways to make fibres into threads and fabrics. These techniques include spinning, **weaving**, knitting and knotting.

Threads and **textiles** can be used to make many things. Warm knitted clothing made from wool offers protection from the cold. Light cotton fabrics are used to make clothing for warmer weather. Other items, such as bags and hammocks, can be made by knotting threads together.

# From fibre to thread

Look closely at a fabric and you might see the fibres it is made of. Wool fibres are thick and warm. Silk fibres are soft and fine. The differences between fibres are easier to see when looked at through a **microscope.**

A close-up view of cotton fibres.

A close-up view of wool fibres.

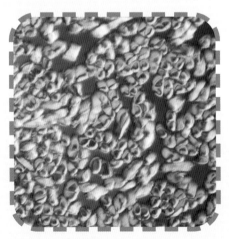

A close-up view of silk fibres.

A close-up view of synthetic fibres.

Natural fibres such as cotton and wool are very short. Before they can be woven into cloth, the fibres must first be twisted together to make a long thread or **yarn**. This process is called spinning. Spinning links the short fibres together so they will not pull apart.

People have been spinning fibres for more than 10 000 years. At first, they simply rolled the fibres together by hand. Then, around 7000 BC, they began using a simple machine called a distaff and spindle. Much later, a wheel was added to help the spinning process. This machine was called the spinning wheel.

In 1767 a machine called a spinning jenny was invented. This made the process of spinning much faster. Today most threads are spun by machine.

These Miri women are making cotton thread by twisting fibres together into a distaff.

This woman is spinning wool on a spinning wheel.

# Chapter 2

## Weaving

Once fibres have been spun into long threads, the threads can then be made into cloth. Even though most of the fabrics used today are made by machine, the process is the same as hand weaving.

Women in Guatemala weave very intricate and traditional patterns by hand.

A close-up view of a woven fabric.

There are two sets of threads used in weaving. These are called the **warp** and the **weft** threads. The warp threads run the length of the cloth. The weft is then threaded through the warp, under and over, under and over. This links the threads together to make a fabric.

Weaving is done on a frame called a **loom**. The loom is designed to make the process of weaving faster and easier.

Silk thread is being made into fabric using this loom.

# Make a meat-tray loom

Follow these steps to make a woven placemat.

## What you need:

- a clean polystyrene meat tray
- wool (one colour, or different colours)
- a shuttle
- a pencil
- scissors

## What to do:

### Step 1

Draw a line about 2 centimetres inside the edge of the meat-tray all the way around. Now cut along this line and remove the middle of the meat-tray.

### Step 2

Tie a piece of wool from the top edge to the bottom edge of the meat-tray.

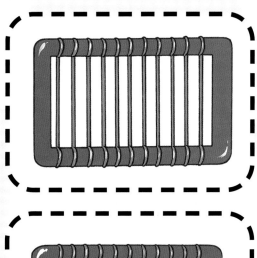

## Step 3

Continue tying separate pieces of wool all the way along until your meat-tray loom looks like this. These are the warp threads.

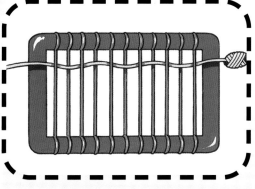

## Step 4

Tie one end of a long length of wool to your shuttle. Starting at one end, thread the shuttle under the first warp thread, then over the next, under and over and so on until you get to the end. This is your first weft thread.

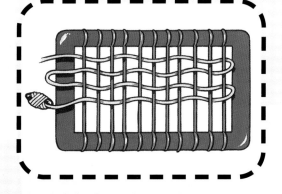

## Step 5

Turn your shuttle around and weave back through all the warp threads again. Remember that if you went under the last warp thread on the line, you need to go over it when you go back the other way.

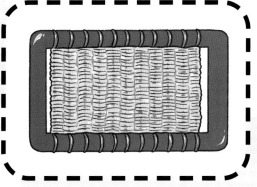

## Step 6

Continue weaving weft threads until you have completed the fabric. To finish, tie the end of the weft thread to the warp thread. Now you can cut away the meat-tray to leave a fringed placemat.

# Chapter 3

## Knitting

Knitting is the process of making fabric using needles and long threads of spun wool or other yarn. There are natural yarns, such as wool, angora and mohair. There are also synthetic yarns, such as nylon and orlon. Knitting yarns can be dyed different colours.

Knitting began in Africa more than 1500 years ago. Arabs knitted socks using the wool from their sheep. Knitting is now practised all over the world, using many different stitches and designs.

# Patterns in knitting

One of the most famous forms of knitting is known as Aran. In Aran knitting, the different stitches represent the different stages of life.

- The zigzag represents the twists and turns of life.
- The cables represent ropes.
- The ladder represents the climb through life to happiness.

# The stages of knitting

Knitting is the process of making a fabric by looping threads together using a pair of needles. These loops are known as stitches. There are two basic stitches used in knitting: the knit (or plain) stitch and the purl stitch. They can be combined in different ways to create a variety of patterns.

## Casting on

Before you can begin knitting you need to do something called casting on. Casting on provides the first row of stiches on the needle.

## Knit stitch

The knit, or plain, stitch is where you actually begin knitting. It is a process that is repeated across each loop on the needle. This is known as knitting a row.

# Purl stitch

The purl stitch is the other most common stitch used in knitting.

# Casting off

The final stage of knitting is known as casting off. Casting off takes all the stiches off the needle and finishes the edge of the fabric.

# Volunteer knitters

At this very moment, all over the world, there are people volunteering their time to knit for others. These dedicated knitters donate their time and skill. They help groups and organisations.

Volunteer knitters make hats, mittens, blankets, scarves and socks for needy members of the community. Organisations then give the much-needed items to schools, nursing homes, hospitals and other local charities.

As well as providing items for the community, volunteer knitting activities also bring together people with a common interest. Many people see it as a way of getting together and sharing both their time and their skills.

# Penguin sweaters

If you thought that volunteers only knitted for people, then think again. People have been knitting clothing for animals for years. Have you ever seen a dog or a cat in a coat? What about penguins wearing sweaters? It may sound funny, but for some penguins it is a matter of life and death.

One of the world's greatest environmental disasters is oil spills. Oil clogs penguins' feathers and, as penguins clean themselves by preening, the penguins are poisoned. Rescuers wash the oil off so that the penguins won't have to. However, this strips the feathers of their natural oils and the penguins cannot keep warm.

The knitted sweaters cover the penguin from head to toe. They come in all sorts of colours – even football team colours. Volunteers receive a pattern to follow so that the sweater is just the right size.

Volunteers are constantly knitting penguin sweaters so that there is always a supply. Let's hope the penguins never need them!

# Chapter 4

## Knotting

Knotting is another way to hold fibres together. Knots can range from simple to very difficult. While knotting is functional, it can also be very decorative.

Knotted objects have been found among the remains from many **ancient civilisations**. Elaborate knotting of **flax**, **papyrus** and **hide** have been discovered in ancient Egyptian tombs. Even the oldest known sculptures show evidence of knotted fabric. Different cultures also use their own particular knot forms.

A pair of ancient Egyptian knotted leather sandles.

An ancient Egyptian knotted fishing net with terracotta weights.

18

# Macramé

Macramé (*say:* mak-rah-may) is an ancient art form that uses hand-tied knots for decoration. It can be used to make fabric for curtains, or to make accessories like belts and necklaces.

The word macramé actually means 'fringed napkin' in Turkish.

These Malay women are making knotted hanging baskets.

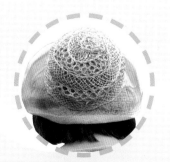

A macramé hat and bag.

# Getting started with macramé

Macramé uses an area, or surface, that is known as a working board. It holds all the threads, or cords, that can be knotted to make macramé.

The mounting cord is the first cord used in macramé. It is attached to the top of the working board and holds the other cords. The working cords hang from the mounting cord. Macramé knots are made around a cord known as the knot bearer. The filler cords are like the knot bearer, but they run down the centre of a series of knots.

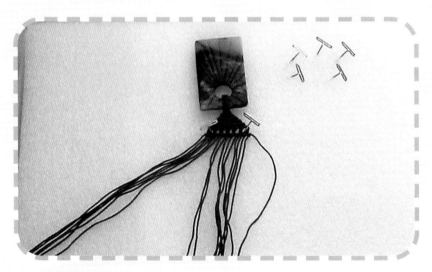

A working board.

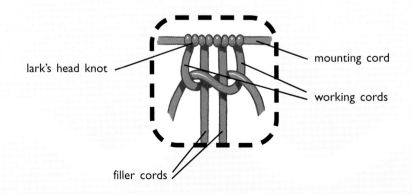

lark's head knot

mounting cord

working cords

filler cords

# Half knot

The half knot is the simplest macramé knot. It can be made beginning with either the left or the right cord.

1. Take the right working cord over the filler cords and then under the left working cord.

2. Take the left working cord behind the filler cords and then loop it forward over the right working cord.

# Square knot

A square knot is made up of two half knots: one beginning with the right working cord, the other beginning with the left working cord.

1. Make one half knot beginning with the right working cord. Then take the left working cord in front of the filler cords and behind the right cord.

2. Complete the square knot by looping the right working cord behind the filler cords and then towards the front over the left cord.

A series of square knots makes a flat braid. When a half knot is repeated it makes a spiral.

# Chapter 5

## Being creative with fibres and fabrics

Fibres and fabrics can be used to make clothes and furnishings, and other useful items such as fishing nets, hammocks and tennis nets. Fibres and fabrics can also be used to make beautiful artworks.

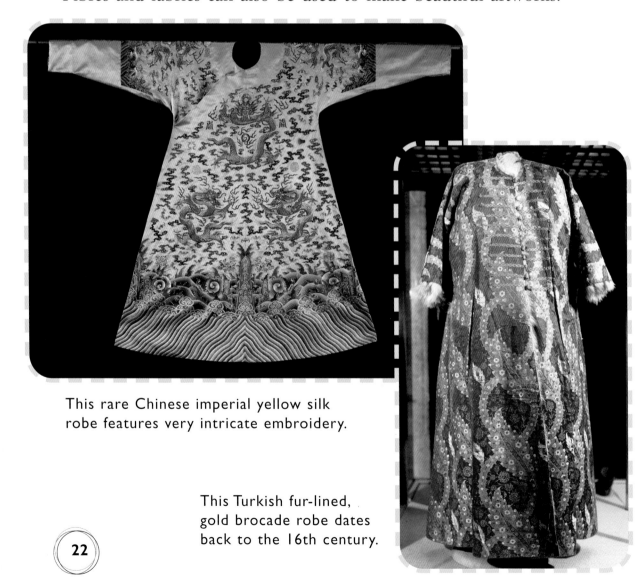

This rare Chinese imperial yellow silk robe features very intricate embroidery.

This Turkish fur-lined, gold brocade robe dates back to the 16th century.

# Working to design briefs

People who work creatively with fibres and fabrics often have a design brief to work from. To make sweaters for penguins, knitters need a pattern. They also need threads to suit the purpose.

A costume maker for the theatre might be asked to create an evening dress for a character on stage.

You could design and make a knotted net for a basketball hoop. Perhaps you could even make a knotted hammock.

You might like to design and make a fabric wall hanging that represents the natural environment.

# Glossary

| | |
|---|---|
| **ancient civilisations** | very old cultures that lived a long time ago |
| **fibres** | tiny strands or threads |
| **flax** | plant fibre from the flax plant |
| **hide** | an animal skin that is treated and used as a fabric |
| **loom** | a frame on which weaving is done |
| **microscope** | an instrument needed to look at very tiny objects |
| **natural** | from nature |
| **papyrus** | a material like paper made from water reed |
| **synthetic** | a human-made substance, not natural |
| **textiles** | materials made from threads |
| **warp** | fixed threads that run along the piece of cloth that is being woven |
| **weaving** | the process of making fibres into fabric by winding in and out |
| **weft** | thread that is woven in and out of the warp threads to make cloth |
| **yarn** | a spun thread |